WHAT IS THE KISMET OF GOD?

SOUTH KAILASH - THE REWRITTEN HISTORY

I'M NOTHING

Clever Fox PUBLISHING

Chennai • Bangalore

CLEVER FOX PUBLISHING
Chennai, India

Published by CLEVER FOX PUBLISHING 2026

ISBN: 978-93-7500-766-1

ABOUT THE AUTHOR

I'm not the special person. I am an ordinary person, just like everyone else. I work for an IT company. I'm an "otrovert" personality person. I have never been greedy for money or assets, and I firmly believe in justice. I'm the empathetic person who doesn't hurt even mosquitoes or ants. I always prayed for the welfare of others. During my teenage years, I was an atheist. My first spiritual fast began on the hill of Sabari (Sabarimalai) to pray for the child's recovery from a bike accident. Sabari Hill is located in Kerala, India. Thereafter, I prayed and pursued the Sabarimala fast for a woman who had previously undergone an abortion for medical reasons to be blessed with a healthy pregnancy. Since then, I have developed strong feelings of love and respect for all pregnant women and developed a habit of praying for every pregnant woman I come across to have a safe delivery and wonderful life for the infants. I wrote a mantra for Lord Sabari and, with God's grace, recited it on all 18 steps of Sabari Hill. I have also written poetry and mantras for the gods (HanuRam, Ayyappa, Jesus, Muruga, Allah, and Shiva) out of love and devotion. I do not see any discrimination between gods. I love and respect all religious deities. People view gods from various perspectives. Some individuals perceive God as the god, while others see God as their father, mother, friend, enemy, and even the troublemaker. I regard God's as my children's, and this perspective has fostered a non-prejudiced mindset in me, and also, I took responsibility for the desires of god's. God's desires are to protect justice and build a joyful and magnificent world. Like everyone else, I'm doing my best to promote justice. The reason I'm discussing only the positive elements of myself is to provide you all confidence in what I'm about to say through my writing.

ABOUT THE BOOK

This book discusses the history of the Velliangiri Mountains (South Kailash), human chakras, the relationship between the Sadhguru Isha Foundation and the Velliangiri Mountains, Mahashivratri, scientific insights into luminiferous ether, God's kismet, and the names of the gods Shiva, Parvati, Allah, Vishnu, and Jesus. Did my pilgrimage rewrite the ancient history (Puranas) of the Velliangiri Mountains? My conversation with God, the effect of prayers, and poetry for God.

I believe the first few pages of this book will be thoughtful, and then it will be captivating, emotional, thrilling, mysterious, suspenseful, and finally divine.

CONTENTS

ABOUT MAHASHIVRATRI

Mahashivratri is celebrated as "***the night for awakening the human chakras and spiritual energy***." Shivratri takes place on the fourteenth day of each lunar month. Among the twelve Shivratris that occur in a calendar year, Mahashivratri falls between February and March. The human body has always had a profound connection to nature and the planets. The smallest moment of planetary shift will have an effect on the human body and mind. The Earth's average radius is 6,371 kilometers (miles). Humans could not survive if the Earth's radius shifted substantially, as a smaller radius would increase gravity, potentially crushing us, while a faster revolution would rip up the surface. If the Sun moves much closer to Earth, solar radiation will be increased, and it would trigger a runaway greenhouse effect, boil the oceans, and turn Earth into a burned, uninhabitable rock. The world would instantly freeze if the sun suddenly moved away from Earth. The lunar eclipse, solar eclipse, full moon day, and new moon day all have an effect on the human system. Our body and mind have a close connection to the planets. It's not only about planets; human life will be impossible if the insects, aquatic organisms, animals, and plants disappear. Even if humans are extinct, insects, aquatic life, animals, and plants can persist. All of these organisms existed long before the emergence of humans. The most dependent organism on this planet is us, "the humans."

For example, ***our ancestors advised us not to go to the sea on full-moon and new-moon days. Why?***

The moon has a significant influence on the Earth's tides. The moon exhibits an influence on the human body, mind, and emotions. Some people experience increased restlessness and mood swings on "New Moon day" due to the lack of moonlight. On both New Moon (Amavasya) and Full Moon (Purnima) days, the sun and moon align, allowing their gravitational forces to merge. This arrangement produces the greatest tides, known as spring tides. The human body is 70% made up of water. So it's not only the seas; the human body's water is also affected by the spring tides, which harm our organs and minds. ***This phenomenon is the reason that our ancestors advised us not to go to the sea on full and new moon days.***

Let's return to the topic of Mahashivratri night. We all know that the Earth orbits the sun in an elliptical orbit. There are two elliptical orbits: smaller and larger. When the earth goes from the larger elliptical route to the smaller elliptical path, Mahashivratri occurs. The northern hemisphere of the planet is positioned in such a way that there is a natural increase in "luminiferous ether" energy in humans.

What is "luminiferous ether"?

Sound energy flows through the medium called air; what is the channel for light energy? People believed that ***light energy required a medium***, which they dubbed the "luminiferous ether," but they were unable to verify the presence of ether energy; therefore, they decided that light did not flow through any medium. ***Luminiferous ether is known as "supreme power," "cosmic energy," and "holy spirit" in different civilizations.*** During the fourth century BC, Aristotle made several discoveries on luminiferous ether, and Newton and Einstein gave it several names. ***Ether is a source of energy that keeps the Earth running in a steady rhythm***. This ether energy is present throughout space and reaches Earth every second. Luminiferous ether is a substantial source of extraordinary invisible energy that flows abundantly toward the Earth, especially at high speeds during Mahashivratri.

What is the difference between the monthly Shivratri and the Mahashivratri?

Ether energy is classified into two types: spring and autumn (seasons). Shivratri in February and March is a spring festival with increased energy and power. To say it in simple words, every second, ether energy falls down on the earth at the speed of a bicycle. ***During monthly Shivratri, ether energy will move at the speed of a flight, and on Mahashivratri, it will fall down on the earth at the speed of a rocket.***

The earth, moon, and sun will align in a straight line during Mahashivratri, which is expected to occur between 12:15 and 12:45 a.m. At this point, the ether energy will be at its peak; this time will vary by country.

Why should we be awake on Mahashivratri night?

The premise of being awake on Mahashivratri day is that if we keep our spine erect and stay up all night, we will be able to get a lot of this rare stream of cosmic energy. Animals and birds lack a **vertical spine**, whereas **human anatomy** has a vertical one. Ether rays will enter our pineal gland via the upper Sahasrara Chakra, aiding in the production of oxytocin (happy) hormones, and it will be best to be in the sitting position and pay some attention to the Shiva devotional mantras to receive the divine energy.

Is it possible to experience the same power during the "daytime" of the Mahashivratri?

No, you can't feel the same cosmic power in the day as in the morning. The sun's rays dilute the ether rays. At night, these ether waves will help us feel connected to the universe. So it is best to sit straight from 9 p.m. to 2 a.m. on Mahashivratri.

Why is Shivratri celebrated solely in India and not in other countries or religious cultures?

People are largely unaware of this tremendous energy, and religious culture restricts people from accepting and experiencing this divine energy. This Ether is known as Eashan or Shivan. Ether Rathiri = Esahan Rathiri, which equals Shivaratri. ***Shiva is not just the Lord's name; the five-letter word "Shiva" symbolizes the five earth elements: earth, water, fire, air, and space. It is preferable to be awake during Mahashivratri, regardless of any religious beliefs or atheism.***

- ***According to ancient (Puranas) legend,*** **Shiva performs the cosmic dance of creation, preservation, and destruction on the Mahashivratri night.**
- According to the ancient Puranas, **Mahashivratri is the day Lord Shiva and Goddess Parvati married, marking their union.**

The ancient Puranas correspond (match) with scientific findings about luminiferous ether, demonstrating the existence of holy cosmic energy on Mahashivratri night.

ABOUT THE VELLIANGIRI MOUNTAINS (SOUTH KAILASH)

Velliangiri, which translates as "**Silver Mountain**" in Tamil language (velli = silver, giri = mountain), is so named because its peaks are frequently shrouded in heavy mist and clouds, giving them a silvery aspect. We can see whitish clouds moving near the base of the seventh mountain. It is also known as the "***Kailash of the South***," and it is sacred to Lord Shiva. The Velliangiri mountains are located in Coimbatore, Tamil Nadu, India. It's part of the Nilgiri Biosphere Reserve. The seven hills, with peak altitudes ranging from approximately 1,778 to 1,850 meters (roughly 5,800 to 6,000 feet), are bordered by the plains of Coimbatore district to the east, the Palghat district of Kerala to the west, the Nilgiri mountains to the north, and the Siruvani hills to the south. The Neelivaikal, Mayar, and Andisunai rivers traverse the steep topography. Lord Shiva is revered as a self-created

(Swayambhu) lingam. The five naturally formed Shiva Lingas (Panchalingas) represent Brahma, Vishnu, Rudra, Maheshwara, and Sadasiva, and correspond to the five earth elements. The hills are rich in natural resources and herbs. The trek entails passing seven unique undulations, which are commonly linked to the human body's energy centers. The first and seventh hills are considered most difficult due to their steep elevations. The rocky steps on a few Velliangiri mountains were built by Ottan Sidhhar, who attained Samadhi on the Velliangiri Fifth Mountain. The Navagraha, also called the nine celestial divine influencers, refers to a different set of celestial bodies: the Sun, Moon, five planets (Mars, Mercury, Jupiter, Venus, and Saturn), and two lunar nodes (Rahu and Ketu) that have a connection to the human body and mind.

At Velliangiri Temple, the Navagraha is made up of a single stone, which is found nowhere else in India. The best time to trek this peak is between February and May. Many yogis and siddhas, including those descended from Saint Agastya, have experienced Samadhi here. The region is inextricably linked to Isha Foundation because it is where Sadhguru's guru attained Samadhi. Sadhguru established the Isha Yoga Center in the foothills of the Velliangiri Mountains because he sees the range as a very spiritual region. Sadhguru teacher Sri Palini Swami attained samadhi and chose to abandon his physical body in the Velliangiri Mountains. The enlightened Sadhguru detected spiritual energy in the Velliangiri Mountains, which is why the Isha Yoga Center was built opposite the Velliangiri foothills.

Thank you, Sadhguru and the Isha Foundation, for your efforts to raise human consciousness, save soil, and create a righteous environment.

According to spiritual tradition, each hill of South Kailash represents a chakra. The Hills 1–6 represent the chakras Mooladhara, Swadishtana, Manipooraka, Anahata, Vishuddhi, and Agnya. The 7th hill signifies the Sahasrara chakra (the highest level of consciousness).

1. Velliangiri First Mountain: Mooladhara (*root chakra*)

The Muladhara chakra (Root Chakra) is positioned near the base of the spine. It is symbolized by a lotus with four petals and the color pink or red. The mantra is "LAM." The element of the Muladhara (Root) Chakra is Earth. The Muladhara mainly represents passion, strength, survival, and a connection to the physical world. The tailbone (coccyx) is the final bone at the end of the spine. It is the only body portion that remains intact after death. It cannot be destroyed, even when burned at high temperatures. The tailbone is intimately associated with the root chakra.

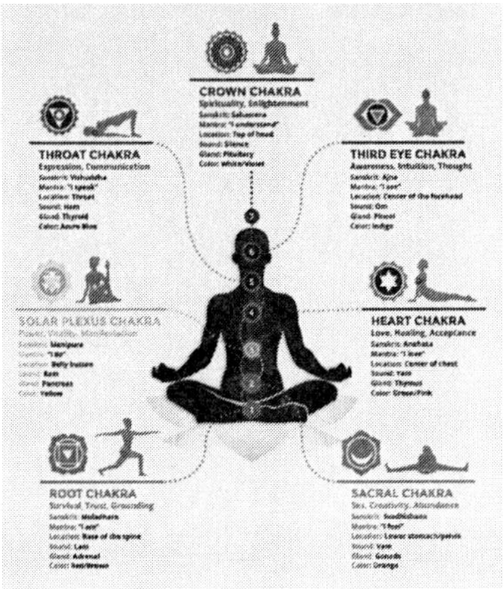

7 Chakras in Human body

The first hill of the Velliangiri mountain is a steep, stair-heavy ascent that leads to the destination, the Vellai (White ash)

Pillayar (Ganesha) temple and is associated with the root chakra. It serves as the starting point for the seven hills. The first hill is the hardest of the seven because of its steep incline. It is generally completed in under an hour and 40 minutes, contingent upon your speed.

2. Velliangiri Second Mountain: Swadhishtanam (*Sacral Chakra*)

The Swadhisthana Chakra, or Sacral Chakra, is the second primary energy center located in the lower abdomen. It is located above the pubic bone and near the sacrum. It's related to the color orange. The mantra is "VAM." The Sacral Chakra (Svadhisthana) element is Water. It represents creativity, sexuality, emotions, and pleasure while also reflecting the flow of life, adaptability, and the subconscious mind.

The Pambatti Siddhar cave and water spring (sunai) can be found on Velliangiri's second hill and is associated with the Swadhishtanam chakra. It is well-known for its bamboo woods and slippery rock stairs, known as Valukku Parrai. It is typically considered simpler than the first. It has several slick spots and will take 1 hour and 15 minutes to complete.

3. Velliangiri Third Mountain: Mani Poorakam (*Solar Plexus Chakra*)

The third fundamental energy center, known as the Manipura Chakra or Solar Plexus Chakra, is located above the navel. It governs personal power, self-worth, confidence, metabolism, digestion, willpower, and transformation. It resembles the color yellow. This chakra is linked to the element of fire and the mantra "RAM."

The third hill on Velliangiri Mountain represents Manipura and is distinguished by a lemongrass landscape. It's difficult terrain includes broken steps, steep dirt paths, and stones. On the third mountain, we can view several types of butterflies. The little shops are situated on the third Velliangiri hill, which ends at the Kai Thatti Sunai (Sunai means spring water or natural spring water found in hilly or rocky areas). It will take 1 hour and 15 minutes to complete. It is an important rest stop before proceeding to the upper mountains.

4. Velliangiri Fourth Mountain: Anahatham (*Heart Chakra*)

The Anahata Chakra (or Heart Chakra) is the body's fourth fundamental energy center, located in the center of the chest. It serves as a link between our physical existence (lower chakras) and our spiritual selves (higher chakras). It combines emotions, allowing for intense sentiments, healing, and selfless love. It represents love, compassion, and connection. It is connected with the color green. The mantra is "YAM." The element of this chakra is air.

The fourth hill in the Velliangiri mountains is connected to the Anahatham chakra. It represents the transition from dense forest to open mountain, with pleasant winds. We can see the views of the Adiyogi statue from the mountain peak. It is rather flat in comparison to the preceding steep slopes; however, climbing over boulders is required due to the lack of official steps. It will take 1 hour and 35 minutes to complete.

5. Velliangiri Fifth Mountain: Vishuddha (*throat chakra*)

The fifth chakra, or Vishuddha, is located in the throat. It controls communication, self-expression, truth, and creativity, and serves as a link between the lower and upper energy chakras. The throat chakra color is blue. The mantra reads "Ham." It is connected with the element of space.

The fifth hill in the Velliangiri Mountains is called Thiruneer Malai (Hill of Sacred Ash) because it has a distinct white, ash-like sand. It is also known as Beeman Kali Urundai because of a rock formation thought to be where Bhima (Character in Mahabharata history) prepared and ate clay balls to satisfy his hunger while the Pandavas remained here during their exile and left the leftover balls. This stretch is very flat and picturesque, with a big round stone lying past the Kai Thatti Sonai (natural spring water). It is regarded as one of the simplest mid-stage climbs. It is related to the mythology of Sita doing penance. It is generally completed in under an hour and 10 minutes.

6. Velliangiri Sixth Mountain: Ajna (*third Eye chakra*)

The Ajna Chakra, also known as the Third Eye or Sixth Chakra, is the human body's principal energy center. It is situated between the eyebrows. This chakra is indigo in color and is associated with the mantra "Aum." The element of the sixth chakra (Ajna/Third Eye) is light. It is related to wisdom, intuition, clarity, and heightened awareness. This chakra is thought to assist people in grasping the truth of the soul beyond the physical world.

The sixth hill in the Velliangiri Mountains represents the Ajna Chakra. It has the Aandi Sunai (water spring) and the Sethizhai cave. It is a little difficult because of the downhill-to-uphill hike portion. It entails climbing down and then up, making it physically challenging. It serves as a rest stop with a holy pond before the seventh hill. It has a natural water stream where devotees typically take a sacred bath in this pond. The pond contains a magnificent shivalinga. This pond is the final major stop before the challenging seventh hill. It will take 1 hour and 35 minutes to complete.

7. Velliangiri Seventh Mountain: Sahasrara *(crown chakra)*

The seventh chakra, also known as Sahasrara or the Crown Chakra, is the highest energy center on top of the head. The color violet represents the Sahasrara Chakra. The mantra is "AH," which means silence. It signifies the element of thought and cosmic energy. It represents pure consciousness, spiritual connection, enlightenment, and oneness with the universe. It serves as the source of divine wisdom and cosmic consciousness. This chakra also gives you a sense of the realization that you are a soul in a human body. The seventh hill of the Velliangiri Mountains, known as the "Kailash of the South" is the final, steepest peak and home to a sacred Swayambhu Shiva lingam at around 6000 feet. The seventh mountain has extremely low temperatures, biting cold winds, and heavy mist, especially at night. I strongly recommend woolen clothing, sweaters, and blankets due to the intense cold. The summit is famous for the location where Sadhguru Shri Brahma attained Mahasamadhi. Lord Shiva is revered as a self-created (Swayambhu) lingam.

The ***five naturally formed Shiva Lingas*** (Panchalingas), which represent Brahma, Vishnu, Rudra, Maheshwara, and Sadasiva, correspond to the five earth elements. The peak of the rock on the seventh mountain will resemble both the Velliangiri deity and Nandi. It will take 1 hour and 55 minutes to complete; however, it may feel much longer because of fatigue. It will be both tough and divine.

The seven sands in the mountains will each be of a different color. The Velliangiri mountains terrain is uneven and rocky. It lacks proper, safe staircases throughout the trek, making the climb, especially the descent, risky. ***The forest officials highly advised individuals with underlying health conditions (heart difficulties, high blood pressure, diabetes, and asthma) to avoid this journey, and all pilgrims should travel in groups, remain hydrated, and be physically prepared***. It happened that some people perished during the journey, and in the last three years, more than 30 people have died while trekking.

Please take care of your health and follow a healthy lifestyle before starting the journey. In total, it will take a maximum of 18–23 hours to trek and descend in the Velliangiri Mountains, and it completely depends on people's physical health and climatic conditions.

Kismet of God:

The word "kismet" originates from the Turkish. It represents fate, destiny, or fortune and is often used to describe events that seem predetermined or destined to happen. **In simple words, "kismet" means fate or**

destiny. In Islam, it often means Allah's will; it means some events are "meant to be." It is important to distinguish this from "karma," which is based on actions, while kismet is generally viewed as an external, predetermined, or uncontrollable force. In addition to literature, Kismet has found its place in Turkish religious practices and rituals, where it represents the divine will of the higher powers. My life is running according to the program that is written by God. ***"Kismet of God" refers to the concept of divine destiny, fate, or a preordained portion in life determined by a higher power***. It suggests that certain events, particularly serendipitous or significant ones, are "written in the stars" or appointed by God. Essentially, "Kismet of God" refers to surrendering to a higher, divine guidance over one's life journey.

Let's see, what is the kismet of God and mine in South Kailash?

My Experience in the Velliangiri Mountains (South Kailash):

Anyone who went to the Velliangiri Mountains would have had an amazing spiritual experience. The enlightened Sadhguru also talked about his spiritual journey and the rationale behind the construction of the Isha yoga center close to the holy Velliangiri mountains. I'm writing this book out of devotion to share about my amazing experience with Shiva at the Velliangiri Mountains.

I believed in God. I repeat that I believed in God. Let me explain what happens to my belief.

How did my South Kailash pilgrimage started?

On Jan 29, 2022, at my home, I spotted the Rudraksha malai (garland) in the concrete slab and inquired about it with my parents. Hello, Mother. Who owns this rudraksha garland? My mother replied, "This rudraksha malai has been used by my late ancestors for many years, and my father's grandmother, who was considered a saint, daily chanted the Gayatri mantra with this rudraksha malai (garland)." ***The moment when I touched that rudraksha garland. I got goosebumps and was interested in wearing it. I donned it after chanting the Maha Mrityunjaya Mantra*** (***Aum|Tryambakam|yajaamahe|sugandhim|pushtiv vardhanam|Urvaarukamiva|bandhanaan| mrityormuksheeya maamritaat*** |) and sent a photo of myself wearing a rudraksha garland to a buddy in the WhatsApp group. My buddy inquired about the hike to Velliangiri mountains after noticing my devotion. Hey, my dear friend, Are you interested in joining us on the Velliangiri hike? I replied, "Velliangiri" is a name I had never heard of before. Where is it located? My friend replied. It's in Coimbatore near the Isha Yoga Center.

I agreed to join their troop for Velliangiri hiking because I felt it would be enjoyable and that the hike would be similar to the Sabarimala hills short route (chinna pathai). I was also excited to visit Isha Yoga. I told another buddy about my excursion to the Velliangiri Hills. I informed him that I was planning to visit the Velliangiri Mountains with a known friend troops on March 1, 2022. They said they are also planning three days after my date of visit, March 5. I told them. Let me join with you as well.

My friends were all shocked and asked. How can you hike twice the time in two days of break? It's impossible, and you are not an athlete, and you are working in an IT company where there is a lack of physical activity. I replied, "Hey, I have strength and stamina, and I go to the gym regularly." I also went to Sabari hills, and so all will be very easy for me. I will take care of myself and accomplish it. I explained to them to give my friends confidence and to allow my friend groups to take me with them as well. I was planning for a joyful experience with friends and thought the trekking would be straightforward.

When I told my parents about my plan to go hiking in Velliangiri, my mother inquired, "**Do you know the history of the Velliangiri mountains**?"

I said, "No, Mother," and this was the first time I had heard the name of the Velliangiri mountain. My mother then told me a short history of it, which I later investigated on Google and understood in detail.

History of Velliangiri Mountains (South Kailash):

Once upon a time, there lived the demon Banasur, and he attempted to conquer heaven and the Himalayas. He was a compelling demonic king. He practiced penance towards Lord Brahma to become immortal. Lord Brahma, pleased by Banasur's devotion, arrived and informed all beings born on Earth that they would die, making it impossible to offer the blessing of immortality. Banasur understood Brahma's statement about immortality and subsequently changed his request for a boon to specify that only a teenage girl could cause his death. Banasur thought he was smart by thinking women were weak, particularly teenagers, and that they would be unable to defeat him. He received a boon from God (Lord Brahma), which stated that only an adolescent girl could cause his death. In Santana Dharma (Hinduism) ancient history, gods will also offer boons to the demons. The granting of a boon by God is based on the efforts and penance of the individual, not on their character. However, God will punish the people and demons if the boon is misused. Lord Shiva is the empathetic as well as the fiery god. Lord Shiva also, pleased by Banasur's devotion, granted the Asura king Banasur a thousand-armed body, immense strength equivalent to thousands of elephants, and personal protection. Shiva also vowed to defend Banasur during the battle. Banasur arrogance grew as he received his boons. Goddess Parvati (Lord Shiva's wife) admonished Banasur for utilizing the boon to disrupt the serenity of the innocent people and the lords of heaven. The devas (lords of heaven) went to Lord Vishnu (protector of the universe) for help, and he said Parvati must incarnate as a virgin teenage girl to demolish Banasur, as that is the only way to slay him (**only the virgin teenage girl is capable of killing Banasur**). The yagya (a sacred Vedic ritual of offering) was developed and accomplished with the aid of saints, and Goddess Parvati is now reincarnated in southern India as a teenage girl named Kumari.

As time passed, Banasur discovered that the virgin teenage girl Kumari had incarnated as Parvati to kill him, and he insisted that she get married to him as quickly as possible. Kumari has been doing penance since her childhood to marry Shiva. The demon Banasura learned of Kumari's existence and fled with his soldiers to kidnap the adolescent girl. Kumari, understanding the situation, went on to seek Guru Prataya's advice on how to defeat Banasur, and meanwhile Banasur desperately searches for Kumari. Kumari decided to perform her penance while standing in order to attain the blessings of Lord Shiva and marry him. Kumari started her penance. **Kumari, at her zenith of devotion, set up a deadline: 'If I am not married to Shiva by sunrise on this day, I am going to leave my soul from the body.'** Lord Shiva came to know about the Kumari penance and hurried down from the Himalayas, while all the other gods conspired against him. The gods thought that if Shiva got married there, he might not return, which would allow Banasur to conquer both the Himalayas and the world. Lord Vishnu and other devas planned to prevent Shiva from meeting Kumari.

Shiva arrived in the southern part of India, where all the other gods were creating distractions to prevent him from meeting Kumari. When Shiva was just a few kilometers from the place where the maiden Kumari was doing penance, the gods created a false sunrise by setting up a massive mound of camphor. Kumari believed that the sun had risen and Shiva didn't arrive to marry her, and she failed in her devotion. Kumari was heartbroken as she believed that she failed in her penance. Banasur arrived at Kumari's place and made fun of her and attempted to marry her. Kumari became enraged, transformed into Adishakti, and killed him. However, Kumari felt that she failed in her devotion and desire to marry Shiva, and in her disappointment, she tossed the wedding food, which turned into the multicolored sand and pebbles. ***The virgin Kumari left her soul from her body in the standing position.*** The place is still known as Kanyakumari. Shiva felt disappointed and upset with himself for not arriving on time. Shiva climbed through the mountain, known as the South Kailash or the Velliangiri Mountains, to release his frustration and arrived at the peak of South Kailash Mountain. **Lord Shiva was not sitting at the peak of the Velliangiri, also known as South Kailash Mountain, in a state of joy or meditation. Lord Shiva sat here with depression, anxiety, grief, heartbreak, tears in his eyes, and anger about himself.** He stayed there for quite some time. After his presence, a self-manifested Shivalinga appeared at the peak of the Velliangiri mountain, and now all devotees are worshipping it.

After hearing about t*he history of the Velliangiri Mountains. Like everyone else who read it, I began to worry and cry over lord Shiva's heartbreak*. There are numerous histories in which God's cried for their loved ones, and that's a quality of being God.

Questions arising in my mind:

I wasn't expecting the story of emotional pain, and a few questions came to my mind. ***How can people worship and seek blessings while God is depressed?***

I pray for you and your entire family and friend's well-being. Assume your parents, friends, or family have lost a loved one and are suffering. ***Do we seek blessings from people who are experiencing heartbreak and suffering? Is it possible for people who are grieving to bless and grant boons?***

No, we will care about them and look for possibilities to get them out of the sufferings. No matter if it's God, when someone is in a state of grief, they need care.

These thoughts were arising in my mind. Whoever is suffering, only requires love and care. I thought it wasn't appropriate for this form of Shiva to reside in the Velliangiri mountains. I planned to bring Shiva down the mountains and reside in my Shivalinga. ***My thoughts sparked feelings and increased my devotion.***

I had one Shivalinga, which I had recently purchased during the Navaratri celebration. ***I'm speaking about it to myself. "Let me go to the Vellaingiri Mountains to rewrite the history by making Shiva and Kumari (Parvati's incarnation) marry. If that isn't possible, I will consolidate Shiva from the Velliangiri mountains to my newly purchased Shivalinga and take excellent care of him for the rest of my life.***

I'm not sure why I developed the superstitious thoughts. It may seem childish and silly, and indeed it is a silly imaginary thought. I also realized that when we have an unlimited amount of love and care for someone, we can perceive the impossible as being possible. Since that day, various forms of Shivalinga have appeared in my thoughts, and I have been obsessed with Shiva. In my imagination, I also transformed Lord Vishnu's conch, Sudarshana Chakra (discus), mace, and lotus into the shivalinga.

I began my trek to the Velliangiri Mountains (South Kailash).

The first pilgrimage to the Velliangiri mountains during Mahashivratri night:

On February 28, 2022, we traveled to Coimbatore via private bus. I kept my thoughts and the reason for the pilgrimage a secret from my friends. My entire focus was on Shiva and my pilgrimage plans.

I took the shivalinga I had purchased with me and took a vow.

"Never lay down my shivalinga on the Vellaingiri Mountains. Always retain the shivalinga in my hands, and do not give it to anyone until the pilgrimage is

complete. If it falls down, Shiva is not coming with me, and then my pilgrimage would be considered a failure."

When I step into the Velliangiri Temple, I feel a sense of peace and reverence. I took a shower and ate a small meal. I prayed to the Lord's and decided that regardless of what happened, I wanted Shiva and Parvati to be together and happy. Shiva should not live in the mountains with broken hearts. I want to modify the history. I transmitted these thoughts to my shivalinga: "Either consolidate Shiva into my shivalinga or change the history so that Shiva and Kumari (an incarnation of Parvati) can be together." Let Shiva and Parvati be together and happiest on the Velliangiri mountain! Let Shiva and Parvati be together and happiest on the Velliangiri mountain!

We decided to start the Velliangiri first mountain walk on February 28, 2022, at 2:30 p.m., but I had stomach pains and diarrhea three times before the event started. **I've exhausted my physical energy and am really tired.** I arrived healthy but turned out to be sick. One of my friends was annoyed since several of the troop members had already begun hiking, and my illness was causing him to delay his journey to the Velliangiri Mountains.

My devotion extends beyond the limitations of my ailing body. At 3:00 pm, I stepped onto the first mountain after praying to Navagraha (nine planets) and Manonmani Amman (deity). ***Despite the difficulties I faced, my vow to bring Shiva and Parvati together was strong. I want Shiva to reside in my Shivalinga, or alternatively, I wish to see Shiva and Parvati marry and live happily together.*** I climbed the mountain slowly, without energy but full of devotion. The walk is difficult, and my health has deteriorated gradually. I wasn't expecting such a lengthy distance. After the first mountain was completed, the priest in the Ganesha temple glanced at my shivalinga and said, "Hey man." Where did you buy this shivalinga? Would you mind giving the shivalinga to me, and I shall do Pooja by keeping this shivalinga over here? I refused to give, and at the same time, I felt worried about being unable to satisfy the priest's desire. When I arrived at the third mountain, one of my buddies made fun of me for my turtle walk, slow progress, and tired appearance. ***He chuckled sarcastically at my fatigued look and inquired, "Will you come back to the Velliangiri (South Kailash) hiking after two days?" I replied to him with an emotional promise while carrying my Shivalinga that I would absolutely return on March 5th for the second trek with my other friend's troops to the Velliangiri Mountains.*** On the way to my pilgrimage, as I looked at the Velliangiri mountains, I spoke to myself, "Oh Shiva, where are you? Please come with me. I'm here to relieve your suffering. I won't let you feel sad. My friend asked me why you are always holding the shivalinga and aren't even willing to give it to me, and many people looked at me with surprised expressions. I'm the one who is carrying the shivalinga on my hand and trekking. I refused to give it to anyone, and I kept telling myself that I should not place it on the ground at any moment. If so, my pilgrimage has failed. I made it to the center of the fourth mountain by Shiv's grace. **I hit a small stone on my foot and fell down on the fourth mountain, and *my shivalinga also fell to the ground.*** I already lost physical energy, and my shivalinga also fell on the ground. I started feeling immense stress and was convinced that my pilgrimage had failed. The negative thoughts began to flood my mind. Despite experiencing severe agony and being overwhelmed by negative thoughts, I did not share my anxiety with my friends and continued my pilgrimage by carrying back my shivalinga. My pals planned to sit on the sixth mountain for dinner and leisure. They were all eating food, and I refused to accept it. I am already broken inside and don't know how to communicate it.

My friend is telling other people about my trekking adventure. He told my other friend, "He is unfortunate; Shiva tested him and subjected him to numerous hardships." I gradually isolated myself from my friends' group and started climbing the seventh mountain. When I came alone from the group, I couldn't bear my misery and began expressing it. My health was deteriorating, and I was unable to intervene because my emotional mind was also in distress. ***Depleted of both physical and mental energy, I took a seat on a medium-sized rock near the base of the seventh mountain.*** I lay down, wrapped myself with a blanket, and cried uncontrollably. I clearly recall when one of my troop members approached me and spoke to me. He was concerned about my health and asked, "Hey, what happened? I'm worried about your health." I covered myself with the blanket and tried not to cry, but I responded to him by asking him to continue his journey. I assured him that I would come back after some time. ***I sat down, sliding my back against a medium-sized rock on the seventh mountain. I was crying a lot while holding my shivalinga and looking at the path I traversed.*** I was terrified (afraid) of my return, feeling severely sad and crying a lot since my shivalinga had fallen down, and I didn't have the energy to climb back up to the seventh mountain or descend to the first mountain. I vowed to return on March 5th, but this promise will also be broken. I failed as a devotee. ***My tears are spilling upon the shivalinga I am holding.*** I spoke to my shivalinga while in profound emotional distress over my inability to complete my pilgrimage.

I spoke to my Shivalinga. ***Oh Shiva, "I am sick and unable to continue my trekking; my legs are***

cramped, and I lack the strength to proceed." Oh Shiva! "My mental health has also been destroyed. I am experiencing enormous tension, stress, guilt, demotivation, despondency, and fear." My emotional pain slowly turned to anger, and I started scolding Shiva. Hey Shiva, "I came looking for your happiness, but you caused me to experience profound heartbreak. "I don't like you anymore. Oh, goddess Parvati, look at Shiva. "How much suffering did he make me experience in this pilgrimage?" My physical energy is drained, and my shivalinga fell down to the ground. "I failed in my pilgrimage; I failed in my pilgrimage." During my pilgrimage, I experienced a profound sense of failure. I hate myself for the inability to complete the pilgrimage. I keep on repeating the same thoughts to myself: My devotion failed. "I lost." I don't have energy in my body or in my mind. Hey Parvati. I hate Shiva; I don't like him. I came for his happiness, and here he gave me the extreme amount of pain in my life. "I do hate myself and my thoughts," I said to myself. How stupid was I to think of bringing Shiva into this shivalinga, and how foolish was I to think of bringing Shiva and Kumari (an incarnation of Parvati) together and changing the history? Oh, it's all my superstitious, delusional, and hallucinatory thoughts that made me feel the extreme amount of emotional pain. I keep on repeating to myself. I'm the idiot; I'm the stupid one. How did I develop superstitious thoughts?

It's all my imagination that put me through the difficulty. ***Later, I decided I didn't want to return home; instead, I considered jumping over the side of the seventh mountain to end my life because I felt I had lost my pilgrimage.*** I took the selfie of my tears and pain to let people and my family know I'm no more. Suddenly, my friend from Gujarat called me, and I shared all my pain, fear, and failure with him. He was encouraging me, affirming that I am a resilient individual, and reminiscing about all the kindness I have extended to my friends thus far. I informed him, "I've lost everything." I lack energy and do not enjoy living. I failed to integrate Shiva into my shivalinga. I failed to help Shiva overcome his sadness, and I failed to reunite Shiva and Parvati. Furthermore, I did not achieve my desire to have Shiva bless all the Velliangiri devotees with happiness. My friend later sent me the Shiva reels, including one featuring the Shiva Tandava Stotram.

"***Jatatavigalajjala| pravahapavitasthale| Galeavalambya| lambitam bhujangatungamalikam Damad damad damaddama ninadavadamarvayam| Chakara chandtandavam tanotu nah shivah shivam***" is the song that depicts the fire starting in the Shiva animated video. I looked at the video and ended the conversation, and the tower was also small on the peak. I felt I was unworthy and not the greatest devotee. ***I decided***

to leap from the seventh mountain with my Shivalinga to end my life. My emotional suffering is excruciating. I was experiencing all the emotions of anxiety, guilt, embarrassment, anger, fear, and grief. My anger at Shiva turned to compassion.

I apologized to Shiva with tears in my eyes for not being able to accomplish my pledge and pilgrimage. I spoke to my Shivalinga with tears, "I have decided to end my life, Shiva, and I can see the path that leads to jumping off the seventh peak, which is about 20 steps away." I failed to unite you and Kumari (Parvati's incarnation). I failed to bring you back from the sufferings. I failed to make you bless devotees in the happiest state of mind from these Velliangiri Mountains. I have decided to end my life, and please at least accept my soul, Shiva." I was looking for Nandhi in my backpack to accompany the shivalinga and prepare myself to jump off the peak. In my search for Nandhi, I touched the Vibhuti, the holy ash that I had taken from home. It was March 1, 2022, at 12:50 a.m. ***It's Mahashivratri night***. I got shivers all over my body after touching the holy ash. I can notice the changes in my body and mind. ***I applied the Vibhuti (holy ash) to my face and placed a kumkum (holy red powder) on my head***. I'm feeling the changes in myself; I stood up with my stick. My body was shaky and then turned to stiffness. I took a step forward toward the seventh mountain and said, "Shiva and Parvati should always be happy and together." This time, all I chanted was, "Shiva and Parvati should always remain happy and united," throughout the seventh mountain. When I utter that particular phrase ("Shiva and Parvati should always remain happy and united"), ***I feel a surge of strength in my body and mind.*** During my adolescence, I was hesitant to keep Vibhuti (holy ash) on my forehead, and for the first time, I applied it all over my face and felt complete tranquility and strength.

I texted one of my buddies with a photo of myself hiking the seventh mountain. I texted him that I would be alright, and he should not search for me. I arrived at the 7th mountain with holy ash all over my face, and when I saw the Velliangiri god, I shouted "Aum Namah Shivaya" louder and louder. I am accustomed to a loud voice, and when I shouted "Aum Namah Shivaya," the people around me joined in, causing the name of Shiva to echo throughout the entire seventh mountain. Later, I sit in the closed-eyes position for about two hours in the chilly air, with my Shivalinga in my palm and just a few meters from the Velliangiri temple god. I continued chanting "Aum Namah Shivaya" afterwards; at some point, I stopped reciting and gradually felt a complete absence of thoughts in my mind. ***I did not feel my physical or emotional presence. My thoughts are idle.*** I knew my thoughts were empty only after they had temporarily become filled with stories of the Velliangiri mountains history. It was roughly 4:30 a.m. I have seen my presence in different dimensions of the universe that I had not seen before.

My physical body is located on the Velliangiri seventh mountain, while my causal or spiritual body, which is one of the three bodies in the human system (physical, emotional, and causal), exists in a different universe. The causal or spiritual body is often described as the "shell of a tamarind seed" that binds the soul to the world. I felt the energy rise in my spine and comprehended why I had these thoughts (to bring the Shiva and Kumari (Parvati) incarnations together), as well as my purpose in these Velliangiri mountains and on this planet.

This time I___ and the sun rises and felt____ rewritten the history. It was around 5:00 am, and in my meditation, I saw Shiva was married to Parvati and united. My closed eyes welled up with tears.

Lord Shiva is not speaking, but the below thoughts are being communicated to my mind.

- ***You came to see me and Parvati getting married and staying joyful and together. Now you see, "We are united and happy!"***
- ***You also had the desire to see me blessing the devotees in the happy state of mind at these Velliangiri Mountains. Look over there, "I am blessing the devotees with happiness."***
- ***You also had the desire to have me reside in the shivalinga that you are holding on your palm. As you wished: "I'm in your linga also to protect you."***

I opened my eyes in tears, the shock lingering in my memory. I'm speechless. I wasn't happy, sad, or emotional, but I felt something else beyond words. **I determined that it was not my imagination, and it's neither a mental illusion causing me to imagine to calm myself and get relaxed from stress. Sometimes our depression**

might force us to utilize our imaginations to get out of it, but this moment felt real to me, not like an illusion. It is an experience that I cannot describe. I admitted that Shiva and Parvati are united, and Shiva blesses his devotees with a joyful state of mind in the Velliangiri Mountains. I gently descended from the mountain with blissfulness. I felt healthy and emotionally robust. At the bottom of the first mountain, I spotted my friend's gang. They were stunned. The person who was worried about me was startled by my return and commented, "You were very weak on the mountain, and I was worried about how you'd return." I told him, "I no longer believe in God's existence." "I know God exists," and by Shiva's grace, I'm back. I returned home after completing my first Velliangiri pilgrimage and kept my Shivalinga in my prayer room.

The second pilgrimage to the Velliangiri mountains during Mahashivratri night:

On March 4, 2022, from my house, I began my second pilgrimage to Velliangiri. I told my friends' group that I would climb alone and began trekking with my Shivalinga. The following day, March 5, 2022, at 3:00 pm, we arrived at the Velliangiri temple to begin our hike. As previously said, during my first-time pilgrimage, the priest desired to have my shivalinga perform prayers at the Velliangiri first mountain Ganesh temple. I bought the ***identical type*** of Shivalinga from the store. I intended to present the identical Shivalinga to the priest at the first mountain. I have arrived at the first mountain but couldn't find the priest there, so I placed the Shivalinga near the Ganesha deity. I feel a force tugging me forward. I hiked up to the sixth mountain with ease. I paused for a bit at the base of the seventh mountain and realized my phone was lost. I assumed that I had been sitting on the 6th mountain for quite some time; I would have certainly left my phone near the rock. I was upset about the loss of my phone because it contained images of my Velliangiri trip, tickets, contacts, and lots of data. These days, phones have become indispensable. ***I felt overwhelmed and anxious due to the loss of my phone.*** I told myself, "Let's complete the pilgrimage soon, as it is very important, and then search for the phone while climbing down from the mountain." I accelerated my trekking pace on the 7th mountain. I collapsed and realized as I was traveling back to the sixth mountain that I was on the wrong path. ***While walking hurriedly, I fell and cramped my leg muscles.*** The leg spasm was getting heavier, and I was unable to walk.

Thank you to the devotees who supported me by giving me the painkiller tablet and water. I took a painkiller, but still I'm not seeing the reduction in my pain while walking. Every step I take causes intense pain because my knee muscles cramp. I shared my lost phone story with one of the Shiva devotees, and he tried calling my phone; ***I heard my phone's ringtone and realized that it had fallen into a hidden area of my bag***. I felt, "Oh, how stupid I am for not checking my bag properly." Somehow, I managed to reach the seventh mountain and worshiped the Velliangiri deity. I was feeling elated about completing the pilgrimage twice and achieving my vow. I took some rest on the seventh Mountain. It's wonderful to see the moon and stars from Velliangiri (South Kailash) seventh mountain. In the early morning, the sunrise was beautiful, and I took some photos. The pain in my knee intensified as I was descending the mountain. I settled near the big rock at 5th Mountain, as I couldn't step in anymore. I texted my parents that I would be late arriving home. ***I spotted a couple of my buddies from my troop on the fifth mountain. I shared my story and muscle cramp***. I requested them to leave and not wait for me since I had muscle cramps. One of my buddies assured me that we would never desert you alone. We will both carry your hand on our shoulders and take you for a leisurely walk.

I was experiencing severe knee pain and ***repeatedly said, "Aum Namah Shivaya," "Jesus," "Muruga," and "Allah" with every difficult step.*** When I utter "Allah," people stare at me with amazement. I have never affiliated with a religion and have no prejudices regarding God.

All of the devotees watched my struggle to get down, and several of them offered assistance, for which I am grateful. Meanwhile, I kept my Shivalinga safe in my bag. ***I arrived at the first mountain with God's grace and the support of my friends.*** At the first mountain, I was stepping down in a sitting position since my leg was in excruciating pain. "I persevered (never gave up)," and "my two friends didn't leave me in any situation." My friend's gang was waiting for us for quite a long time. Finally, I descended from the Velliangiri mountain and prayed to the goddess Parvati. In my prayers, "I thanked all of the gods, including Jesus and Allah, as well as my friends, for their presence and support throughout my pilgrimage." After concluding my prayers, I experienced a surge of strength in my leg. ***I began walking regularly and springing from the steps like a horse.*** My friends couldn't believe it and were fatigued from carrying me on their shoulders. I am saying to my friends, "Hey, my leg feels good." I can't describe the beautiful moments and events that are taking place in words. I reached my home safely along with my Shivalinga.

The rise of my enlightenment:

After my two pilgrimages to the Velliangiri mountains, I felt a new transformation in my life. I fasted for the first time during Ramadan to thank Allah and all other god's for helping me during my Velliangiri pilgrimage.

I began writing a book entitled "The Father of ___ and the ____ for Human Emotions." The thoughts focus on ***the questions and answers around "Who is God?" and "Where is God?" Who created humans? Who created God? Why isn't God coming to save humanity? Why are there so many different gods?, etc. ?The book contains definitions and explanations for life, religion, lifestyle, birth, education, friendship, marriage, movies, politics, money, career, parenting, death, rebirth, heaven, hell, and soul. The book also explains about thoughts, emotions, and the _____ for each human emotion.***

I confined my thinking to 108 queries. This book answers all of the questions that people have concerning their daily lives. I had never read a book before and never imagined myself as a writer. **My head was flooded with all of those questions and answers, and I had a goal and vision of getting this book (*The Father of ___ and the ___ for Human Emotions*) into the educational system**. It will bring humanity together and help them thrive on the path of righteousness (Dharma). I also came up with the idea of constructing a temple for the gods of all religions. The Hindu temples, Christian churches, and Muslim mosques should all be built in the same compound. ***All should have unique entrances and the***

same exits. I would like to see all religious people united as they leave the compound.

I have also begun my Mahadev Jyotirlinga pilgrimage and traveled across India. I have visited Kedarnath, Somnath, Dwaraka, Nageshwar, Mahakaleshwar, Ohm Kaleshwar, Khasi, and Rameshwaram. In six months, I visited seven jyotirlingas, each of which was an unforgettable experience. **I also vowed to never visit the temple without my shivalinga.** At Kedarnath, in -5 degrees Celsius, I meditated for two hours without a shirt, with sacred ashes all over my body and my shivalinga in my palm. People asked how I meditated without a shirt in this frigid weather, and I replied, "I'm feeling heat on my shivalinga." When I am full of devotion to Shiva and holding my Shivalinga, I notice changes in my body and mind.

At Khasi, I fell into the Ganga River and almost plunged 12 feet deeper. ***I do not know how to swim***. I was progressively losing consciousness. I suddenly remembered my talk with my cousin on the journey to Rishikesh. I said to him, "***As long as I have Shivaling in my hands, I feel safe, and death can't reach me.***" I plunged around 12 feet deep into the Khasi Ganga River. I was silently uttering a prayer in my thoughts while holding my Shivalinga in my palm. ***Oh, Shiva, "What's happening? My purpose and goal are incomplete;***

please save me from dying." After that prayer, the Ganga River gradually drew me up from 12 feet to the slanting zone, and a few North Indians asked me a question. Did you take the Shivalinga out of the Ganga River? The boat rider was startled, my Khasi troop was ecstatic, and my parents were delighted that I was still alive. I had the opportunity to perform ceremonial water bathing for the lord Mahakaleshwar Jyotirlinga in Indore, India. I also had the chance to touch the Mahakaleshwar jyotirlinga. I consider it the most powerful jyotirlinga I have ever touched. I experienced complete tranquility.

I'm undergoing so many fantastic experiences with my Shivalinga. ***I recently had cardiac arrest. Two days before the cardiac arrest, I got a thought about this incident during my meditation.*** I even wrote my last will and shared it with my cousin. I didn't give up. I went to the hospital and was having a health check at the hospital, and the doctor reviewed my report and said I was fine with no heart abnormalities. In the hospital, I had an unexpected cardiac arrest.

The doctor did CPR, and I eventually recovered consciousness. When I regained consciousness and opened my eyes, I saw a white mountain for a few milliseconds. The doctor who did CPR to save my life was also pregnant. I am still alive because the cardiac arrest occurred in the hospital, with the help of the pregnant doctor and the grace of God. I'm highlighting my cardiac arrest event because, as I previously stated, I have developed a habit of praying for pregnant women and infants whenever I encounter them on the road or anyplace. ***This little, consistent practice of prayer for pregnant women and infants has saved my life in difficult situations.*** I learned that even the smallest acts of kindness can have a big influence. People around me began referring to me as an enlightened being, someone near to Shiva, and a strange individual, among other titles. I'm still living a normal, ordinary life like everyone else, but my thoughts are led by the grace of God.

In search of myself, I realized that "I'm nothing."

The devotion I have experienced has transformed me into a better human being, and I would define this experience as devotion. Devotion to God alone is not considered devotion; rather, commitments to one's education, job, family, friends, goals, etc. will also be considered devotion. ***Devotion is defined as being fully focused and committed to whatever we are involved in accomplishing.*** Devotion will transform our life once we are committed to it.

The third pilgrimage to the Velliangiri mountains during Mahashivratri night:

The third pilgrimage to the Velliangiri pilgrimage occurred on Mahashivratri night in 2023, and it was the most enjoyable journey. I helped by the grace of Shiva to fulfill my cousin's wish to visit the Velliangiri hills. I gave Shiva Parvati "***my happiness***" as a marriage anniversary gift.

The fourth pilgrimage to the Velliangiri mountains during Mahashivratri night:

The fourth pilgrimage to the Velliangiri mountain occurred on Mahashivratri night, March 8, 2024, and was another wonderful experience. This year, **I made an oath that I would not drink a drop of water until I finished the third mountain. I am going to give Shiv Parvati "my thirst" as a wedding anniversary present**. I went with my pals, and I also told them about my vow. Surprisingly, when we entered the **Velliangiri temple, there was no water**, even for bathing. I felt, "Nature is supporting my vow by creating the thirsty environment." I began the walk with my friends on March 8th at 8:00 a.m., remembering my prayers and committing not to drink water until I complete the third mountain. I've been reciting Shiva mantras in my thoughts while climbing the mountain. My friend advised, "It's a sunny day, and trekking the first three regions of the Velliangiri mountains

without drinking water is impossible and dangerous." I replied that "My thirst" is my gift to Shiva and Parvati's marriage anniversary. I won't give up on my vow. ***During our hike, we discovered that there isn't much drinking water on the mountains. Devotees also claimed that there isn't much water on the mountain, and there was a long queue of people waiting to fill***

their bottles. I rested whenever I could and gradually climbed the mountain.

My body was failing; the sun had sapped all of my physical power, but my devotion remained strong. My friends' gang has already gone to the front, and I have always desired to go alone with my shivalinga. Even if I had intended to accompany the friend gangs, Shiva always distanced me from the gang to experience the situations that I had never encountered before in my life. At the third mountain, I noticed a dog that had been following me for a long time. When I take a break, it stands beside me.

I felt as if "Dog came to support me." I was nearing the end of the third mountain at roughly 5:00 p.m. Suddenly, I stumbled and fell from the mountain while clutching my Shivalinga. I was completely unconscious at the time. ***Although water was scarce in the mountains, the devotees around me gave me drinking water to wake up. When I fell, I saw in blurry vision the white snake in a coiled position. I went unconscious after hearing the snake hissing. I felt anxious because I believed my vow had failed after I drank the water.*** I sat anxiously at the base of the fourth peak for two hours.

After 8:00 p.m., I decided to descend the fourth mountain and told myself, "I lost," "I won't return to the Velliangiri Mountains," and "I'm not entitled to be a Shiva Parvati devotee." While descending the mountain, I distributed my torch light and some money to others in need. I prayed that all of them would complete their pilgrimage joyfully. I told Oh Shiva, "Please bless all of the other devotees. I never want them to feel failure in the pilgrimage." I sat on the middle of the third mountain and decided to take a rest and step down in the morning.

At midnight, I was getting Mahashivratri wishes on my phone. I preferred not to answer messages, but I also wanted to avoid offending anyone by ignoring their text. So I replied to the text messages by sending the shivalinga sticker. Once I sent the sticker, I felt a surge of energy. ***I was packing all my belongings to go to sleep. While packing, I touched the holy ash, which I took from my home. I felt the same vibes again that I felt on the first Velliangiri pilgrimage. I smeared holy ash all over my face. I told myself, "Let me restart my pilgrimage from here." I decided to finish the vow by refraining from water until I reached the fourth mountain.*** The fourth mountain is the most complex, with many huge stones. My stomach is already empty, and my body has no water. With the money I had, I purchased a torch and began climbing from the third peak. I started to feel thirsty.

My tongue is completely drained. I can feel a lack of water in my body. I do remember my visit to Omkareshwar

Jyotirlinga, where I did a deep early morning water meditation in the Narmadha River. ***I recited the name of the Narmada River; I consider the Narmada River as my daughter. I said, "Hey Narmada, your father's energy is dwindling, and thirst is at its greatest. Please protect me until I reach the fourth mountain."*** I have completed climbing the fourth mountain and am now at the beginning of the fifth mountain. I see a boy silently helping by watering the devotees. I requested some water from him, and by looking at my faint face, he provided some quantity of drinking water. ***I drank the water and could taste the essence of the Narmada River in it.*** I felt surprised and gained confidence. I also collected some amount of water from him in the water bottle. I started trekking slowly and could still see water scarcity at the start of the seventh mountain. I eventually reached the 7th mountain by March 9th, at 7:00 am. I recited my prayers while looking at the Velliangiri deity. Oh, my lovely Shiva Parvati. "I have come to give my thirst as a gift for your marriage anniversary." Please accept this gift. I feel tears of joy welling up in my eyes. I am also dancing in my mind for having accomplished the pilgrimage. ***While descending from the seventh mountain, I noticed the excellent amount of water flowing in the sixth mountain (Aandi Sunai River). I inquired of devotees about the water scarcity, and they told me now that the water is flowing well in the mountain's pipes.***

At that moment, **I sensed the acceptance of my gift and devotion**. I also recognized that the Velliangiri mountains also helped me fulfill my vow (my thirst as a wedding anniversary present to Shiva Parvati).

The fifth pilgrimage to the Velliangiri mountains during Mahashivratri night:

The fifth expedition to the Velliangiri mountain took place on Mahashivratri night, February 15, 2026, and was another fantastic experience. It was Valentine's Week. It seemed like a Valentine's day celebration in the Velliangiri Mountains. This year, I vowed that I would not talk until I met the Velliangiri deity on the seventh mountain. I am going to give Shiv Parvati "***my silence***" as a wedding anniversary gift. The silence is the source of creation; hence, it is extremely powerful.

After seeing the Velliangiri deity and completing my silence fasting, I chanted the mantra supplied at the conclusion as the first voice (words). I carried a printout of this book to the Velliangiri Mountains, where I thanked the gods and mountains for supporting me in finishing my writing on time. I successfully completed my fifth pilgrimage to the Velliangiri mountains by the grace of the gods.

My pilgrimage will be continued.

CONCLUSION

Thank you to the gods and the Velliangiri Mountains for transforming me into a better human being. Thank you for my friends and all the devotees who supported me during the Velliangiri pilgrimage. Thank you to all the readers who took time to read my experience. ***The reason to publish the book is to let the world know about my pilgrimage experiences and the existence of God. I can see the increased number of devotees to the Velliangiri mountains in these 5 years, but people are still talking about how Shiva lost his loved ones and traveled to the Velliangiri mountains alone to relieve his frustration. Yes, it happened once, but the history has been altered. The Velliangiri Mountains history that describes how Shiva lost her loved one has been revised and rewritten. Kumari finally won in her penance and married Shiva. Shiva and Parvati are happy and united. Shiva has been blessing the devotees in the joyful state of mind in the Velliangiri Mountains (the Kailash of South India).*** Whatever I have written on the above pages was out of my devotional experience and the grace of God. ***I shared 99% of the truth,***

and for that remaining 1%, "I didn't lie; I simply concealed it." It's not my imagination, an illusion, or a hallucination. I and God, are the proof. "I no longer believe in the existence of God," since in my experience, "I know God exists." Not every ancient historical event can be rewritten. The death of Yeshua (Jesus) established the path of love and Christianity. The separation of Lord Krishna and Radha paved the way for unconditional love. The Mahabharata war happened to uphold justice and provide us with the Bhagavad Gita. Shiva lost Sati during the Satyayuga, which caused him to experience profound anxiety, and it took 1000 years for Sati to reincarnate as Parvati and marry him. ***I did not state that all ancient histories could be modified or rewritten. It is impossible.*** We cannot reverse the wars and suffering that happened earlier in our families, relationships, countries, and around the world. ***Every situation happens for a reason. The situations will improve once we identify and understand them, especially once we develop the ability to transform them into positive outcomes in life.*** The history of the Velliangiri Mountains happened for significant reasons. The grace of the planets and gods has rewritten this history for good reasons. Shiva and Parvati were already together. Now they are united in these Velliangiri Mountains, too. At the Velliangiri Mountains, I sensed the happiness of Shiva, the togetherness of Shiva and Parvati, and the victory of Kumari's penance. ***Many***

people will find it difficult to accept my explanation. People worship gods all day in life but doubt those who say they've seen or experienced God. Doubt is very good because it leads to clarity. People's blind faith (believing without the doubts) has led to numerous wars on this planet. It's necessary to have doubt before believing, and it's also mandatory to get clarity for the doubt. In life, ***the truthful experiences of others will be regarded as either beliefs or disbeliefs until we have that experience.*** Please remember that the first step to experiencing the truth is to have a little bit of belief. Shiva is happy, and Shiva and Parvati are united and happy in the Velliangiri mountains too. It's all enough for me, you, and every devotee.

I'm requesting devotees to follow the below steps while praying to God's.

First, please say, "Thank you to God."

We should be thankful to God for whatever we have in life. Some people do not have the basic essentials that you do, such as hands and legs, a healthy lifestyle, food, shelter, and money. Being thankful for what you have right now fosters a sense of gratitude and encourages you to seek things to be happy about.

Second, "Please pray for God's and God's family happiness."

Like us, God also has a family, and we are all one among the family members. What feelings arise when someone wishes us well-being and prays for us, and how does that bind our relationship? When someone prays for our well-being, it has a profound impact on our relationship. It will make us feel blessed and look at them in love. It raises our confidence in life. It will also strengthen the relationship. Likewise, please pray for God's happiness and well-being too. If you do so, you don't need to seek God; you will become the god-seeking person. It will strengthen your relationship with God and make you feel like a selfless individual.

Finally, "Keep your desires aligned with your prayers."

Please manifest your desires on a daily basis and never forget to put up the necessary efforts. By the grace of God, your prayers will be successful or lead to a wonderful experience.

I wrote a mantra/chant for Shiva and Parvati. I request all the devotees to chant this mantra whenever you are worshipping.

Sanskrit: ॐ मित्रस्य रक्षक लिङ्गेश्वर महावैराग्य भस्म रूप अर्धनारीश्वर नमः शिवाय नमो नमः

Aum Mitrasya Rakshaka lingeshwaraya Mahavairagya Bhasma Rūpaya Ardhanārīśvaraya Nama shivaya Namo Namaha.

Hindi: *ॐ शिवशक्ति जोड़े को शादी की सालगिरह की शुभकामनाएं, मैं आपकी खुशी और एकता के लिए ध्यान करता हूं।*

Tamil: பக்தர்களை நண்பன் போல் காக்கும் லிங்க வடிவரே ! உலகப் பற்றுகள், ஆசைகள் மற்றும் பொருள் சார்ந்த நோக்கங்களைத் துறந்தவரே, சாம்பல் வடிவம் கொண்டவரே, அர்த்தநாரீஸ்வரரே !! ஓம் நமசிவாய ந-நிலம், ம-நீர், சி-அக்னி, வா-காற்று, ய-ஆகாயம் என பஞ்சபூதங்களையும் ஆளும் மங்களகரமான சிவபெருமானை வணங்குகிறேன் 🙏

English: **Aum** – sound of the universe; **Mitrasaya Rakshaka lingeshwaraya** – Name of my shivalinga; **Mahavairagya** – Maha – Great; Vairagya – it denotes a state of being “untouched” by desires, material and sensual pleasures; **Bhasma Rupa** – the form of ash (Vibhuti) representing the impermanence of the physical body; **Ardhanarisvara** – Shiva and Parvati fundamental unity of the consciousness and energy; **Nama Shivaya Namo Namaha** – I bow down to Lord Shiva again and again.

Telugu: భక్తులను మిత్రునిలా రక్షించే లింగాకారుడు! ప్రాపంచిక బంధాలను, కోరికలను, భౌతిక లక్ష్యాలను

త్యజించినవాడా, ఓ భస్మ స్వరూపుడా, ఓ అర్ధనారీశ్వర స్వామి!! ఓం నమశ్శివాయ, న-భూమి, మ-జలం, చి-అగ్ని, వా-గాలి, య-ఆకాశం అనే పంచభూతాలను పాలించే పవిత్రమైన శివుడికి నమస్కరిస్తున్నాను.

Malayalam: സ്നേഹിതനെപ്പോലെ ഭക്തരെ സംരക്ഷിക്കുന്ന ലിംഗാകൃതിയുള്ളവനേ! ലൗകികമായ ആസക്തികളും മോഹങ്ങളും ഭൗതിക ലക്ഷ്യങ്ങളും ത്യജിച്ചവനേ, ചാരത്തിന്റെ രൂപമുള്ളവനേ, അർദ്ധനാരീശ്വരനായ ഭഗവാനേ!! ഓം നമശിവായ ന-ഭൂമി, മാ-ജലം, ചി-അഗ്നി, വാ-കാറ്റ്, യ-ആകാശം എന്നീ പഞ്ചഭൂതങ്ങളെ ഭരിക്കുന്ന ഐശ്വര്യമുള്ള ശിവനെ ഞാൻ നമിക്കുന്നു.

I request all the devotees to chant this mantra on the Mahashivratri night.

Sanskrit: ॐ शिव शक्ति दम्पतीः विवाहस्य वार्षिकोत्सवस्य कामना अहं भवतः सुखाय, मिलित्वा च ध्यायामि

AUM Shivashakti dampatih vivah varshikotsavasya shubhakamana aham bhavatah sukhay, militva ch dhyayami

Tamil Meaning: ஓம் சிவசக்தி தம்பதியருக்கு திருமண நாள் வாழ்த்துகள், உங்கள் மகிழ்ச்சி மற்றும் ஒற்றுமைக்காக நான் தியானிக்கிறேன்.

Telugu Meaning: ఓం శివ శక్తి ఈ జంటకు అద్భుతమైన వివాహ వార్షికోత్సవ శుభాకాంక్షలు తెలియజేస్తూ, మీ ఆనందం మరియు ఐక్యత కోసం నేను ధ్యానిస్తున్నాను.

Malayalam Meaning: ഓം ശിവ ശക്തി ദമ്പതികൾക്ക് മനോഹരമായ ഒരു വിവാഹ വാർഷികം ആശംസിക്കുന്നു, നിങ്ങളുടെ സന്തോഷത്തിനും ഐക്യത്തിനും വേണ്ടി ഞാൻ ധ്യാനിക്കുന്നു.

Hindi Meaning: ॐ मित्रस्य रक्षक लिंगेश्वराय महावैराग्य भस्म रूपाय अर्धनारीश्वराय नाम शिवाय नमो नमः

English Meaning: Aum Shiva Shakti Wishing the couple a wonderful wedding anniversary, I meditate for your happiness and togetherness.

I love all the gods, and I see them as my children's, so "I am free from prejudice." I will not extol myself as the greatest devotee or everyday worshiper of gods. I only visit two or three sacred locations per year. I would say that more than I worship, I love, respect, and care for the gods, whom I regard as my children.

People worship a multitude of gods on this earth. People often worship the gods as their religious community dictates or can choose the god out of love. It's wrong to comment with hurtful words or discriminate against any religious beliefs or god's. Many people unknowingly worship their own superiority complex thoughts instead of God. One shouldn't worship gods with the mindset of "your God," "my God," "the first God," "the best God," "the supreme God," "the servant God," etc. Atheism will be considered better rather than worshipping the God with these attitudes.

1. **Which religion is best to follow?**
2. **Which god is supreme, powerful, and the best?**

If you didn't ask these two questions while worshipping God, that's the "BEST" for you, your devotion, and the environment. Believing in God, religion, or anything is dangerous if it leads to superiority complex, arrogance, discrimination, or a conquering attitude. Believing in God, religion, or anything is best if it promotes equality, unity, love, and an inclusive attitude. Most of the wars in the world have occurred and continue to occur because many people exhibit a superiority complex while practicing their religion.

Religion means bringing "discipline" to human life. If we inject a superiority complex in the religion, then it will poison the mind and environment and also the religion we practice. Hating and spreading hatred against other gods will result in the God we worship hating us. ***No human is superior (upper class), and no humans are considered inferior (lower class) because of birth,***

money, assets, and religion. The qualities only decide whether we are upper or lower class.

Please vividly remember, if we consider ourselves to be superior because of birth, money, assets, and religion, then our qualities will be considered very inferior.

Every father and mother will naturally take responsibility for their children's well-being and work hard to fulfill their children's desires. I too took responsibility for the desires of my children (God's). As you are all aware, the desire of God is to bring unity among people and spread love and peace and uphold justice. **When the good and evil are in equal proportions, that will make the environment and life balanced**, but unfortunately nowadays the evil has arisen much more than the good in the minds and actions of humans. Throughout history, people have fought many wars over religious views, and such events continue to occur today. People set themselves apart in the name of God and religion. When someone causes harm to other religious people and attacks their gods, people think that it is not everyone's problem. People claim that God exists everywhere, yet they refuse to accept other forms of God, causing separation and strife among religious groups. Nowadays, even in social media comment sections, people are spitting harsh words at each other in the argument about the gods. The parents always wish to see their children united and together. I'm not God, but I am the father of the gods, so it hurts me when people fight and criticize other deities and religions. My children stand together, but people who worship them are divided. As I previously stated, religion is discipline, but people's brains are warped by superiority complexes and conquering thoughts, and that is making religion poisonous. Many people are suffering from superiority complex disorder. People desire for their life, family, state, and country to be the best, which is acceptable; however, achieving these goals should not involve making other people's lives, families, states, and countries worse.

"Religions are the best" is a reasonable statement. "Only my religion is best" is a perilous claim. Please read this quote and choose the one that best fits your life and situation, then change your viewpoint accordingly. When religious teachings contradict environmental well-being, they must be revised to align with contemporary understanding of sustainability and the importance of protecting our planet for future generations, as failing to do so can lead to detrimental consequences for both the environment and society. It's not only about religion but also politics, movies, ads, lifestyle, education, environment, and most importantly, human physical and mental health must all be revised in order to make a magnificent environment.

Why are there so many gods?

I will write an answer to this and all questions related to God, life, birth, death, education, marriage, children, siblings, friendship, money, emotions, rebirth, death, soul, etc. in my next book.

Let's have a look at my poetry and mantras. I wrote poetry and mantras for some of **my children** out of love. I believe it is poetry, and those who follow and worship their respective religion's gods will enjoy it.

My poetry to Allah.

I wrote this while waiting for the crescent moon visibility to appear in the sky to start Ramadan. After I completed this poetry, I got a call from the courier delivery person, and I received the holy Quran as a present from my friend.

English language:

As-salamu alaykum wa rahmatullahi wa barakatuh.

Allahu Akbar, my morning arises by listening to the Fajr prayer, and Your divine name "Allah" enters into my consciousness through the ears.

I chanted Your name, "Allah," more than I called the name of my mother.

Allahu Akbar, whenever I am pronouncing Your name, You have raised the oxytocin in my heart.

Allahu Akbar, Oh Allah! you gave the book called the Quran to the world through the recipient and the messenger, Prophet Muhammad.

The Quran.

Humans need a soul to breathe in life. The soul enters heaven by reciting and following the Quran.

Ramadan is the month the Quran was revealed to the world. It marks the day humanity was freed from darkness and entered the light.

Like Mecca with its never-ending holy water, the love of Allah will be an unquenchable lamp for everyone.

Insha Allah. Happy Ramadan!

Tamil language:

அல்லா செவிகளின் மூலமாய் என் நினை வாற்றலுக்குள் சென்றாய்.

உச்சரிப்பின் வாயிலாக உள்ளத்தை ஆட்கொண்டாய் .

நான் அம்மா என்று அழைத்ததை விட அல்லா அல்லா என்று உங்கள் பெயரை அழைத்தது தான் அதிகம்.

நபிகள் நாயகம் உள்ளத்தின் வழியாய் குரான் என்ற புத்தகத்தை உலகிற்கு தந்தாய்.

குரான் !!

மனிதன் வாழ்வதற்கு காரணம் அவனுள் இருக்கும் உயிர்.

அந்த உயிர் உன்னதமான நிலை அடைந்து உயர உதவுவது அல்லாஹ வின் வார்த்தை யை புத்தகமாய் கொண்ட குரானின் மூலம் .

ரம்ஜான்- குரான் உலகிற்கு உதித்த நாள் .

உலகம் இருளில் இருந்து மீண்டு ஒளி அடைந்த நாள்.

என்றும் வற்றாத புனித நீர் சம் சம் கிணறு கொண்ட மெக்கா போல அல்லாவின் அன்பும் அணையா விளக்காய் அனைவர்க்கும் இருக்கும் .

இனிய ரமலான் நல்வாழ்த்துக்கள்.

Arabic language:

السلام عليكم ورحمة الله وبركاته. الله أكبر، يشرق صباحي بسماع صلاة الفجر، ويدخل اسمك الإلهي «الله» إلى وعيي عبر الأذنين. رددت اسمك «الله» أكثر مما ناديت باسم أمي. الله أكبر، كلما نطقت اسمك، قمت برفع الأوكسيتوسين في قلبي. الله أكبر، يا الله! لقد أعطيت الكتاب المسمى القرآن للعالم من خلال المتلقي والرسول النبي محمد. القرآن. يحتاج الإنسان إلى روح ليتنفس في الحياة. تدخل الروح الجنة بتلاوة القرآن واتباعه. رمضان هو الشهر الذي نزل فيه القرآن

للعالم. إنه يمثل اليوم الذي تحررت فيه البشرية من الظلام ودخلت إلى النور. ومثل مكة بمياهها المقدسة التي لا تنتهي، فإن محبة الله ستكون مصباحًا لا ينطفئ للجميع. إن شاء الله. رمضان سعيد!

My Poetry to HanuRam:

Hanuman is famous for the Ramayana, an ancient Indian epic that tells the story of Lord Rama and Sita. Hanuman symbolizes courage, strength, gratitude, companionship, and, most importantly, dedication.

I wrote a poetry on the occasion of Hanuman's birthday and changed the name from Hanuman to HanuRam.

Tamil language:

அஞ்சனையின் அஞ்சா புத்ரரே, சீதாராமனை இதயத்தில் சுமக்கும் அன்பான பக்தரே,

ஜகத்தை ரட்சிக்கும் ஈசனின் சிஷ்யரே, சக்தி தேவி யானா பார்வதியின் வீர ஸ்வரூபரே. "நடபுக்கும் பக்திக்கும் இலக்கணம் உடையின் அவை சொல்லும் உங்கள் பெயரையும், புகழையையும்.

அனுதினமும் உங்களை அணைக்க விரும்பும் ராமனும், ராமபக்தர்களின் சேனையும்" ;

அகிலம் உங்களை அழைப்பதோ ஹனுமான் ஆனால் , நீங்களோ உங்களை அழைக்க பட விரும்பவுவது " ஹனுராம்".

ஹனுமான் என்று அழைக்காதீர் ஹனுராம் என்று அழையுங்கள். ஹனுமானையும் ராமரையும் நாமத்தால் இணையுங்கள். அதுவே, ஹனுமானின் விருப்பம். "தன் பெயரிலும் ராமநாமம் தன்னை அனைத்து இருப்பது."ஹனுராம்!! ஹனுராம்!! ஹனுராம்!!

English language:

Oh son of Anjana, oh beloved devotee who carries Sitaram in his heart, oh disciple of Shiva who saves the world, the language of friendship and devotion symbolizes your name and fame!

"Rama and the army of his devotees want to embrace (hug) you every day." The universe calls you Hanuman, but you want to be called "Hanuram.

"Hey devotees, please do not call him Hanuman; call him Hanuram. Join Hanuman and Rama by name. This is the wish of Hanuman. "Even in his name, the name of Rama has to be included."

Jai sree Hanuram!! Hanuram!! Hanuram!!

I wrote a mantra for Hanuman in the Sanskrit language.

"***Aum Anjanai putraya vidmahae sitaram Bhakthaya dheemahi thano HanuRam prachodayat."***

Aum HANURAM namaha.

ॐ अञ्जनै पुत्रायः विद्महाए सीताराम भक्ताय धीमहि थानो हनुरं प्रचोदयात्।" ॐ हनुरे नमः ।

Meaning;

Aum - Sound of universe; **Anjanai putra**- son of Anjanai ; **Vidmahae**--To know or understand; Sitaram Bhakthaya--Greatest devotee of Sitarama ; **Dhimahi**--worship or mediate; **Thanno**--- stimulate; **HanuRam** -- New name of Hanuman as a symbolize of friendship (Hanuman + Raman = HanuRam); **Prachodayat**- To inspire

Hindi language:

हे अंजना के बेटे, हे प्यारे भक्त जो सीताराम को अपने दिल में बसाते हैं, हे शिव के शिष्य जो दुनिया को बचाते हैं। हनुमान दोस्ती और भक्ति की निशानी हैं।

"राम और उनके भक्तों की सेना हर दिन आपको गले लगाना चाहती है।" दुनिया आपको हनुमान कहती है, लेकिन आप "हनूराम" कहलाना चाहते हैं।

"हे भक्तों, प्लीज़ उन्हें हनुमान मत कहो; प्लीज़ उन्हें हनूराम कहो। हनुमान और राम के नामों को मिला दो। यह हनुमान की इच्छा है। "उनके नाम में भी राम का नाम शामिल होना चाहिए।"

जय श्री हनूराम!! हनूराम!! हनूराम!!

Telugu language:

ఓ అంజన కుమారుడా, సీతారాముడిని హృదయంలో మోసే ప్రియమైన భక్తుడా, ప్రపంచాన్ని రక్షించే శివుని శిష్యుడా, స్నేహం మరియు భక్తి అనే భాష నీ పేరు మరియు కీర్తిని సూచిస్తుంది!

"రాముడు మరియు అతని భక్తుల సైన్యం ప్రతిరోజూ నిన్ను కౌగిలించుకోవాలని (కౌగిలించుకోవాలని) కోరుకుంటాయి." విశ్వం నిన్ను హనుమంతుడు అని పిలుస్తుంది, కానీ నిన్ను "హనురామ్" అని పిలవాలని కోరుకుంటుంది.

"హే భక్తులారా, దయచేసి అతన్ని హనుమంతుడు అని పిలవకండి; అతన్ని హనురామ్ అని పిలవండి. హనుమంతుడిని మరియు రాముడిని పేరుతో కలపండి. ఇది హనుమంతుడి కోరిక. "అతని పేరులో కూడా రాముడి పేరు చేర్చబడాలి."

జై శ్రీ హనురామ్!! హనురామ్!! హనురామ్!!

My poetry to Jesus:

Whenever I look at the church. It's become my habitual nature to say by looking at the church "I love you my son" " I love you my son".

Tamil language:

யூதர் குளத்தில் தோன்றிய பெத்லகே நட்சத்திரமே. அன்னை மரியா கைகளில், குடி கொண்டிருக்கும் அன்பின் ஸ்வரூபமே யேசுவ. இயற்கை வரம் அளித்த இறைவனே இரக்க குணத்தின் தலைவனே.

"அன்புக்கும் கருணைக்கும் மாற்றுப் பெயராக இயேசுவை நாம் பெயரிடலாம்." உங்கள் பிறந்த நாள், அன்பின் சின்னம் உலகில் உயிர்த்தெழுந்த நாள்.

அன்னை மேரி உங்கலை வயிற்றில் சுமந்தது 9 மாதங்கள் , அன்னை மேரியின் கைகளில் நீங்கள் அமர்ந்து கொண்டு மக்களை ஆசிர்வதித்து கொண்டு இருப்பது கணக்கிட முடியா காலங்கள்.

தந்தையின் சொல்லை உங்கள் சொல்லாக்கி உலகிற்கு அன்பேணும் தர்மத்தை போதித்தீர்கள்.

உலகத்திற்கு நல் வழி பிறக்க மரணத்தையும் நேசித்தீர்கள். ஒற்றுமை உணர்வின் மூலம் அன்பின் உணர்வை உலகிற்கு வெளிப்படுத்தும் முதல் நாள் இயேசுவின் பிறந்தநாள்.

English language:

The star of Bethlehem appeared in the pool of Jews.

Jesus is the embodiment of love and he love living in the arms of Mother Mary.

Jesus is the God who gave the Bible as a boon to this world and he is a master of compassion."We can name Jesus as an alternate name for love and mercy."

Jesus birthday is the day where the symbol of love is resurrected in the world.

Mother Mary carried Jesus in her womb for 9 months, and he has been blessings people's from Mother Mary's arms countless times.

The words of God (Father) became words of Yeshua, and he accepted death to give birth to love and to create a good path in the world.

The birthday of "Yeshua " is the first day to express the feeling of love to the world through a sense of unity.

"Merry Christmas to everyone."

Hindi language:

बेथलहम का तारा यहूदियों के तालाब में दिखाई दिया।

जीसस प्यार की निशानी हैं और उन्हें मदर मैरी की बाहों में रहना पसंद है।

जीसस वो भगवान हैं जिन्होंने इस दुनिया को वरदान के तौर पर बाइबिल दी, दया के मालिक हैं। "हम जीसस को प्यार और दया का दूसरा नाम कह सकते हैं।"

जीसस का जन्मदिन वह दिन है जब दुनिया में प्यार की निशानी फिर से ज़िंदा होती है।

मदर मैरी ने जीसस को 9 महीने तक अपनी कोख में रखा, और उन्होंने अनगिनत बार मदर मैरी की बाहों से लोगों को आशीर्वाद दिया है।

भगवान (पिता) के शब्द येशुआ के शब्द बन गए, और उन्होंने प्यार को जन्म देने और दुनिया में एक अच्छा रास्ता बनाने के लिए मौत को स्वीकार किया।

"येशुआ" का जन्मदिन एकता की भावना के ज़रिए दुनिया के सामने प्यार की भावना ज़ाहिर करने का पहला दिन है।

"सभी को मेरी क्रिसमस"

Telugu language:

బెత్లెహెం నక్షత్రం యూదుల కొలనులో కనిపించింది.

యేసు ప్రేమకు ప్రతీరూపం మరియు ఆయన ప్రేమ తల్లి మరియ చేతుల్లో జీవించడం.

య్రేసు ఈ పపంచానికి బైబిల్‌ను వరంలా ఇచ్చిన దేవుడు, కరుణకు అధిపతి. "ప్రేమ మరియు దయకు ప్రత్యామ్నాయ పేరుగా మనం యేసు అని పేరు పెట్టవచ్చు."

యేసు పుట్టినరోజు అనేది ప్రేమకు చిహ్నంగా ప్రపంచంలో పునరుత్థానం చేయబడిన రోజు.

తల్లి మరియ 9 నెలలు తన గర్భంలో యేసును మోసింది, మరియు ఆయన లెక్కలేనన్ని సార్లు తల్లి మరియ చేతుల నుండి ప్రజలకు ఆశీర్వాదంగా ఉన్నాడు.

దేవుని (త్రండి) మాటలు యేషువా మాటలుగా మారాయి మరియు ప్రేమకు జన్మనివ్వడానికి మరియు ప్రపంచంలో మంచి మార్గాన్ని సృష్టించడానికి ఆయన మరణాన్ని అంగీకరించాడు.

"యేషువా" పుట్టినరోజు ఐక్యత భావన ద్వారా ప్రపంచానికి ప్రేమ భావనను వ్యక్తపరిచే మొదటి రోజు.

"అందరికి క్రిస్మస్ శుభాకాంక్షలు"

My own Sanskrit mantra to Lord Ayyappa(Sabari Hill)

I wrote a mantra for Lord Sabari and, with god's grace, recited it on all 18 steps of Sabari Hill.

"AUM Dharma sasthaya vidmahae Mohanarudraaya dhimahai Thanno Dhahastha Prachodayat"

ॐ धर्म सस्थाय विद्महे मोहनरुद्राय धीम्हि तन्नो दहस्ता प्रचोदयात्

Meaning ; **Aum** - Sound of universe; **Dharma** - discipline, Justice: **Sastha**-- teacher/guide; **Vidmahae**--To know or understand; **Mohanarudraaya**--Son of mohini & Shiva; Dhimahi--worship or mediate; **Thanno**

--- stimulate; **Dhahastha**-- New name or form of God as a preserver for righteousness; **Prachodayat** - To inspire

My poetry to Lord Muruga(Tamil language):

Lord Murugan is a major deity for people in Tamil Nadu (a State in India) and also in Malaysia and Singapore. He is the son of Lord Shiva and Parvati. I wrote this poetry while I was visiting one of his temples in Thrichandhur, Chennai, Tamil Nadu, India.

நெருப்பில் இருந்து வெளிவந்த நட்சத்திர கணியே, திரிசூலத்தில் நடுவில் இருக்கும் நெற்றிக்கண்ணின் திரு உருவமே, ஆறுபடை வீடு கொண்டு உலகையே காக்கும் மஹேசனின் மைந்தனே, நெல்லிக்கனி யால் உயிர்களின் உடல்நலத்தைக்காக்கும் மீனாட்சியின் செல்வனே, தந்தைக்கு வேதத்தை எடுத்துரைத்த குமரனே, அழகனே, மயில் வாகனனே, சேவல் கொடியே, உன் திருவடியை காண விரைந்தேன் திருச்செந்தூரின் சுப்பிரமணியனே!!! மகிழ்ந்தேன் குமரனின் திருவடியை கண்டு, நெகிழ்ந்தேன் அவன் எனக்கலித்த அருளை உணர்ந்து.

வாழ்வின் இருபக்க மான இன்ப துன்பத்தை உலகிற்கு எடுத்துரைத்தது உன் இரு திருமணம், உன்னை புகழ்வதால் பெருமைப் பெற்றது தமிழ் இலக்கணம்!!. உன்

திருநாமம் ஓசைக் கேட்பதால் ஆழிக்கிணறும் வற்றாமல் அனைவருக்கும் அருள் மழை பொழிகிறது !!!

மர இலைகளை கண்டேன் இலைகள் அனைத்தும் உன் மீது பக்தி கொண்டே, உன் வேல்லின் வடிவத்தை தங்களது திருவுருவ வடிவமாய் தோற்று விட்டது என்பதை உணர்ந்தேன்!

எல்லா உயிர்களிலும் வேலவனாய் பள்ளி கொண்டு அருளும் குமரனே, உலகம்அறிந்தது உன் ஆறுபடைவீடு ஆனால் நீ வசிப்பதோ எண்ணற்ற எல்லா உயிர்களின் உள்ளம் எனும் கூடு !!!

English language:

Oh star-shaped star that emerged from the fire, Oh divine form of the eye in the middle of the trident, Oh son of Mahesan who protects the world with his six-armed house, Oh Selvan of Meenakshi who protects the health of beings with the nectarine, Oh Kumara who explained the Vedas to his father, Oh beautiful one, Oh peacock's vehicle, Oh rooster's flag, I have rushed to see your divine feet, Oh Subramaniam of Tiruchendur!!! I was delighted to see Kumara's divine feet, and I was moved by the grace he bestowed upon me.

Your two marriages have explained the two sides of life's joys and sorrows to the world, and Tamil grammar has become proud of praising you!!. By hearing the sound of your holy name, the deep wells do not dry up, and the rain of grace showers on everyone!!!

I saw the leaves of the tree. With devotion to you, all the leaves have taken the form of your weapon Vel as their own divine form!

Oh son of Shiva, who is the most powerful among all beings, the world knows your six-fold holy house temples, but you reside in the nest of the hearts of all countless beings!!!

Thank you again to everyone for spending your valuable time in reading my book. I wish, pray for and bless everyone for the wonderful life.

I complete my writing for this book with a statement: "Kismet by Grace."

Now, kindly ask yourself and then let me also know. What did you get by reading this book?

By "I'm nothing"

My email ID for communication and clarifications.

writernothing1@gmail.com